Destined For Victory
60 Days of Inspiration

Arkevious Armstrong

Destined For Victory: 60 Days of Inspiration

Copyright © 2018 Arkevious Armstrong

ISBN: 978-1-948829-06-9

First Edition: May 2018

Published by
Greater Working Women Publishing, LLC
www.gwwpublishing.com

10 9 8 7 6 5 4 3 2 1

Marisha,

Thank you for the support and love! Allow this book to move you and inspire you.

ACKNOWLEDGMENTS

Giving a huge shout out to the many people across the world that have allowed me to inspire them through my inspirational messages, videos, and personal interactions. I THANK YOU for allowing me to make a difference in your life. I am truly humbled by the opportunities to use my life experiences to point someone else in the right direction.

INTRODUCTION

Being an Inspirationalist, I discovered three things about the human mind.

1. We need a daily dose of motivation and inspiration.

2. We are in need of daily solutions.

3. We are in constant search of results.

Destined for Victory: 60 Days of Inspiration will do the following things:

- ✓ Encourage you to view situations from different perspectives.
- ✓ Help you to make healthier choices and wiser decisions.
- ✓ Assist you in discovering solutions, sharpening your vision, and guiding you to build courage, so that you can reduce the feeling of conflict towards self.
- ✓ Enliven your desire for self-worth and heighten your accountability.
- ✓ Increase your capacity to achieve results.
- ✓ Deepen your satisfaction and happiness.

Destined for Victory: 60 Days of Inspiration will provide you with the important keys that will help you get your day started with a positive outlook and mindset. Most importantly, it will help you identify and rectify your own issues.

ARKINSPIRE
WEEK 1

"Choose to focus your time, energy and conversation around people who inspire you, support you and help you to grow you into your happiest, strongest, wisest self."

DAY 1

Today you are coming for everything that belongs to you. You are going to be everything they thought you were not going to become.

Trust yourself! Create the kind of self that you will be happy to live every single day. Have faith in yourself. You can, you will, and you should and if you are brave enough to start, you will!

DAY 2

Evaluate you! Self-examine what you are doing that is hindering you from accomplishing your goals.

Courage does not happen when you have all the answers. It happens when you are ready to face the questions you have been avoiding your whole life. Until you become honest with yourself, nothing will change. Nothing changes until you change.

DAY 3

People do not resist change. They resist being changed.

Your mind is just like a muscle: the more you exercise it, the stronger it gets and the more it can expand. The choices you make determine your destiny. Make the decisions that will alter the structure of your reality.

DAY 4

Faith! It is not seeing but trusting God in every step.

Remain authentic, be true to yourself, always believe and have faith in your capabilities. Confidence comes not from always being right, but from not fearing to be wrong. Fear kills faith! Always remember optimism is the faith that leads to achievement.

DAY 5

Today is the day you unleash the beast that is inside of you. Stop suffocating your gift and your potential.

Everyone has inside of them something special. You were born with a gift. No one knows what that gift is BUT YOU! The beauty is that you do not know how great you are until you UNLEASH your true potential. Walk in favor and not fear. Walk with determination and no doubt.

DAY 6

You will succeed!

Tell yourself who you are and what you are capable of every single day. You are powerful and you are mighty. The world will respond to you. What you think of yourself, others will think of you also. Move forward with confidence and courage.

DAY 7

*Your priorities must change and
your expectations need to change.*

Life will discipline and teach you
very valuable lessons when you're
not prepared. So many people
struggle in life because they are
afraid to make the necessary
adjustments that will change their
lives. To have the life you desire to
live, you must prepare for it.

Week 1 Inspirational Journal

How did you exercise your mind this week?

_____

_____

_____

_____

_____

What are your current priorities?

_____

_____

_____

_____

_____

What should your priorities be?

_____

_____

_____

_____

_____

_____

What gifts do you need to unleash?

_____

_____

_____

_____

_____

_____

ARKINSPIRE
WEEK 2

"When you have a dream, you've got to grab it and never let it go."

DAY 8

Stop waiting for the right time or when it is convenient.

You know exactly what it is you want to do. You certainly know what you need to be doing. Procrastination will rob you from all of your energy. Distraction and Procrastination will not only slow you down it will convince you that it is not important.

Get off your butt....

DAY 9

Few reasons why we lose focus on our goals are mainly because of three things:

Lack of desire

Lack of Motivation

Lack of Urgency

Just imagine if you applied these three components to your daily activities

DAY 10

Your Attitude will dictate your altitude!

Look at it like this, put out in the atmosphere what you want in return, you plant positive, you harvest positive. You plant negative, you harvest negative. Having the right attitude and character will open doors and great friendships.

DAY 11

You are what you do repeatedly!

The signs of insanity are doing something repeatedly and getting the same results. The reason why people can never become who they want is that they are too attached to who they always have been.

DAY 12

Take ownership!

Just admit it!! You make more excuses than executions. It is everyone's fault but yours. This is what I need for you to do, get out of your way. Tell that little voice in your head to SHUT UP!! You got this, now let's make it happen.

DAY 13

You've written your goals down repeatedly and made multiple plans to accomplish them. Yet! You've struggled to execute your goals simply because you have become accustomed to making excuses.

Without you putting in the hard work and commitment, it's going to be impossible to finish anything you wish to have. Without discipline and dedication, you're left with just promises and hope. Every decision must follow with action. You must be committed to every action every single day. GET TO WORK!

DAY 14

Everything around you is falling apart. You've lost your grip on life. Nothing is working for you. Giving up seems easy, doesn't it?

You must stay locked in and focused on your target. Trust the process. Those losses you took, you'll bounce back from them. The right people are about to come into your life and connections are about to form. Opportunities are about to be created. Get yourself together. Dust yourself off. Get prepared!

Week 2 Inspirational Journal

✳How did you train your mind this week?

_____

_____

_____

_____

_____

_____

How did you focus on yourself?

_____

_____

_____

_____

_____

_____

How was your attitude?

_____

_____

_____

_____

_____

_____

What did you own up too?

_____

_____

_____

_____

_____

_____

ARKINSPIRE
WEEK 3

*"I don't make excuses,
I make results."*

DAY 15

It is important that you train your mind what to do.

What is consistent in your life; is your life. You are where you are in life because of two things. You either lack the consistency of growth or you are consistent with not trying.

DAY 16

Focus on yourself, focus on the things that you need to work on. Will it get hard? Yes! Will you become discouraged? Yes!

Don't ever give up! Don't ever give in! Don't ever stop trying! Anything that gives you a reason to smile and to live is a reason to dedicate yourself to it every day. That is your purpose.

DAY 17

Commit to your vision and stop robbing yourself.

It is very hard to work on things every single day on a consistent basis. This is a mental preparation. The mind tells the body what to do, the body can't tell the mind what to do. Dedicate yourself and commit yourself to your vision and purpose.

DAY 18

There are some things you will need to change to help you not only become a better person but will help you go to the next level.

All you need to do is focus on the structure of your faith and change your strategy and your approach. Watch how you will go from good to great, from average to phenomenal.

DAY 19

You must fight that voice of doubt and disbelief!

The attack is in your mind. Let go of fear, it will choke your ability to move forward. If you allow it, that voice can become really loud and will distract you from ever taking the first step. I need for you to tune out the noise and speak to your situations and circumstances.

DAY 20

Your desires will keep you going.
Your consistency and dedication will
get you there.

You must not just like what you do;
you must love it, want it and desire it.
You have to have a passion for it.
You need to be infatuated with it.
You have the ability and skills, now
give it 110% every day. You need to
attack your goals with force. You
can't be 50/50. It's all or nothing.
Even when you do not feel like doing
anything, do something.

DAY 21

You must plan, prepare and proceed with confidence.

Life will discipline you if you are not prepared. It is very important that you prepare for all missions. The lack of preparations will always give you short-term results. How do you successfully plan and prepare? You do that by developing discipline. Develop these two habits and they will help you execute effectively.

Week 3 Inspirational Journal

What questions did you face this week that you have been avoiding?

_____

_____

_____

_____

_____

_____

What did you commit too?

_____

_____

_____

_____

_____

_____

What doubt did you overcome?

_____

_____

_____

_____

_____

How will you discipline yourself?

_____

_____

_____

_____

_____

ARKINSPIRE
WEEK 4

"Discipline is the bridge between goals and accomplishments. You can't go to the next level if you're not disciplined in whatever area you're struggling in."

DAY 22

Seize the moment, right now not tomorrow.

Know the true value of time: snatch, seize and enjoy every moment of it. No idleness, laziness, nor procrastination. Never put off tomorrow what you can do today.

DAY 23

Wake up every day with the expectancy of execution. You owe this to yourself. These are your goals, this is your life. You must earn it.

There will be obstacles and challenges. So what! Get started now. Get started with what you have. Every day you must work on it, you will gain progress and confidence as you dedicate yourself to the task.

DAY 24

Your biggest obstacle is doubt. You doubt yourself too much. You focus on the negative and not the positive.

Don't give intimidation an invitation into your mind. Focus on yourself. You will be surprised with how great you really are. You are capable and can do anything you desire. You must develop good habits. Start thinking positive, speak positive and live positive. Listen to uplifting music and watch positive videos.

DAY 25

Stay focused on your goals and not obstacles. If you just focus on what is ahead of you, you will never have time to worry about your past. Your past can not help you get to your destination.

You will need to change many habits. Nothing changes until you change. Change the way you think and you can change your life. You are victorious, you are a champion. I need for you to fix your focus.

DAY 26

What you think or hear the first 30 minutes of your day, normally affects how you start your day.

We can bring positive energy into our daily lives by smiling more, talking to strangers, telling others how amazing they are. Your positive energy will radiate your life, be the game changer, be the thermostat and control the atmosphere.

DAY 27

You are whatever you attach yourself too. You are what you are willing to become.

Put yourself around positive people, and positive energy. You chose your energy, good or bad. Putting forth positive energy connects back to the basics of human values. What are some good deeds that you have done? Know the value of you; like your smile, your energy, your kindness, and your sense of humor. Whatever it is make sure you change someone's life.

DAY 28

You may be lacking confidence, ambition or you may have both but don't have the willpower.

Whatever your passion is, keep doing it. Don't waste time chasing your success by comparing yourself to others. Always excel at doing what your passion is and only focus on perfecting it.

Week 4 Inspirational Journal

How did you seize the moment this week?

_____

_____

_____

_____

_____

_____

What did you expect to happen this week?

_____

_____

_____

_____

_____

What goals did you stay focused on this week?

_____

_____

_____

_____

_____

_____

What do you want to become?

_____

_____

_____

_____

_____

_____

ARKINSPIRE
WEEK 5

"A person's happiness is shown through their actions in life, NOT what they post on social media."

DAY 29

You have to redirect your focus and center your thoughts on your goals.

Focus on what you can gain instead of what you might lose. I need for you to eliminate distractions, not just from other people, but from the things we do to distract ourselves.

DAY 30

You may not be where you want to be or doing what you want to do when you are trying to accomplish your goals.

Confidence doesn't come out of anywhere. You must develop good habits, great qualities, and a strong mindset. You have got to be willing to have vision and foresight that leads you to an incredible end.

DAY 31

If you have lost your fire and desire to pursue your dreams, then your hunger is not there any longer.

What drives you to get up in the morning to chase your dreams? What makes you happy, if you truly want to be in a better position, then you change your habits? There will be situations that come up, you just continue to press through. You are Victorious!!!!!!!

DAY 32

The struggles you are going through today will offer the strength you need for tomorrow.

It is not over yet! If you woke up that means you have another opportunity to achieve your dreams. You have plenty of opportunities and chances in life. Will you always feel your best? No! Just take your shot and have confidence.

DAY 33

Let go of yesterday. You are hurting yourself by holding on to the past hurt.

You can't fix what has already happened. Move forward, focus ahead and start living your life. There are new beginnings ahead, so get ready to embrace them.

DAY 34

You have the potential but you lack the ambition.

You are wonderfully made and created to do amazing things. I need for you to find your WHY that is deep down inside of you to push you to the next level. Find that THING that makes you go hard and allow that to be your fuel.

DAY 35

Too often you have thought about throwing in the towel, NOT YET!!

Just because it is hard, difficult and you can't seem to get a break, you must trust the process. Your break is coming so get ready for it. There is a light at the end of the tunnel.

Week 5 Inspirational Journal

What do you see yourself doing?

_____

_____

_____

_____

_____

Where do you see yourself going?

_____

_____

_____

_____

_____

What are you doing with your potential?

_____

_____

_____

_____

_____

_____

How can you turn your current struggles into your strength?

_____

_____

_____

_____

_____

_____

ARKINSPIRE
WEEK 6

"We get so caught up in life that we forget to live. You will not get a second chance at life. Value and appreciate you more."

DAY 36

Your old habits have kept you in the same place for so long. You have become accustomed to the same behaviors, that you don't see anything wrong.

You need to adopt some new habits. Surround yourself with new peers, positive and driven individuals. Always remember what makes you comfortable will ruin you and what makes you uncomfortable will help you grow.

DAY 37

You have so many great ideas. You have been waiting and anticipating the right moment. GUESS WHAT!!!

You need to continue to plan and prepare. If you don't prepare, you are actually planning to fail. This doesn't necessarily mean you shouldn't act on those very things you desire. What you need to do is develop a plan and get moving.

DAY 38

You have written your goals down and you started working on them. You started out on FIRE.

Three major keys will help you stay focus:

Fixing your focus by locking in on your goals. Write down what is important. Develop the productive habits that will help you execute easily. You did not come this far too only come this far.

DAY 39

Every day is a different day to approach your day in a different way.

What you dealt with yesterday or last week doesn't mean you have to deal with it today. How you perceive your day will dictate how you start and finish it. Think positive and respond with a positive attitude.

DAY 40

Focus on what matters the most to you. Starve the distractions and narrow in on what is important.

One major key is to focus our conscious mind on things we desire not things we fear. Fear is just an emotion, you will eventually get over it.

DAY 41

You become what you think of the most. You respond to what you feel the most.

What you think, you will eventually become. You are shaped by your thoughts. What you get by achieving your goals is not as important as how you become by achieving your goals.

DAY 42

Know your weakness and strengths. Learn to maximize your true potential.

You will feel afraid at times. You will feel weak at times. But remember fear and weakness are not your enemies. There are forms of evolutionary wisdom. Focus on your strengths, not your weakness. Focus on your character and not your reputation.

Week 6 Inspirational Journal

What great ideas are you sitting on?

_____

_____

_____

_____

_____

_____

✷ What bad habits do you need to let go?

_____

_____

_____

_____

_____

_____

What is currently distracting you?

_____

_____

_____

_____

_____

_____

What are your strengths and weaknesses?

_____

_____

_____

_____

_____

_____

ARKINSPIRE
WEEK 7

"If you woke up without a goal, go back to sleep."

DAY 43

When you want to achieve anything that is beyond impossible, the question is how seriously do you want it?

Nothing will ever change in your life nor get better if you stay comfortable. Opportunities and possibilities happen when you step out of your comfort zone.

DAY 44

Lack of direction normally is the reason why many don't move or act on their goals and dreams. It has nothing to do with the lack of time. You have the same 24 hours as Bill Gates.

You may not know where you are going but as long as you know to spread your wings and allow the wind to carry you in the direction you need to go.

DAY 45

The moment you step outside of your comfort zone is when you start seeing growth and change.

When was the last time you did something for the first time? Everything starts changing and growing when you step outside of your comfort zone. Stop being satisfied with Good and start going for Great!

DAY 46

Whenever you want to change you would need to concentrate and stay positive. Focus on your strengths and not your weakness.

Your strengths do not come from winning. Your struggles develop your strengths. Focus on not the situations but your capabilities to turn all situations into great opportunities. You think positive, stay positive and positive things come to you.

DAY 47

You will overcome frustration, just by staying intensely focused on the outcome and not the obstacles.

With hard work, perseverance and self-belief, there is no limit to what you can achieve. Success is determined not by whether or not you face obstacles but by your reaction to them.

DAY 48

Just because the opportunities are not happening right now, does not mean that it won't. Just because you have been doing it for years and see no results, does not mean you should quit.

Never, never, never give in! Courage does not always roar. Sometimes courage is the little voice. You are victorious, you are a winner. Think like a winner and a champion. You are not a quitter. Rise up and Fight!

DAY 49

You have trusted the ones close to you. You have been there for people and supported their goals and dreams.

Today I want you to focus on you, love you, do for you and care about you! Put you FIRST! We can get caught up in doing for others so much that we forget about ourselves. It is time YOU come FIRST!

Week 7 Inspirational Journal

How bad do you want to achieve your goals?

_____

_____

_____

_____

_____

Describe your comfort zone.

_____

_____

_____

_____

_____

What changes are you willing to make today to get you where you need to be?

_____

_____

_____

_____

_____

_____

What opportunities do you believe you have missed and why?

_____

_____

_____

_____

_____

ARKINSPIRE
WEEK 8

"We can't teach our kids to be responsible when they don't see us being responsible."

DAY 50

You got the heart and ability to do some amazing things. You just lack the mentality.

Your happiness depends on your mindset and attitude. There are so many individuals that have the ability to do some amazing things but lack the mentality to keep them there. You need to develop the right character that will allow your mind to take you far.

DAY 51

When determination meets opportunity and when ambition meets the right attitude.

Always know everything happens for you, not to you. Everything happens at exactly the right moment. Learn to have patience; the right time is never when we expect it but always on time.

DAY 52

Life will discipline those who are not prepared for it. You must find out what it is that keeps you from focusing and not executing.

Put your focus on your goals and not on the very things that are keeping you from working on them. How important are your goals to you? You must be hungry and determined to go after them.

DAY 53

Your daily habits will either help you or kill you. Choose which one you prefer to commit too.

Where the minds go; the person will follow. You may have a goal but you are a huge procrastinator. Then you really have nothing. Break the habit that is keeping you from becoming great. Develop the habit that helps you to be great.

DAY 54

External motivation is only a temporary fix.

When you have accomplished your goals and have everything you desire to have and you still are not happy. Outside looking in, you have it all together but within you are broken apart. Find out about your WHY! What gives you life? When you find it, make sure to apply it to your daily activity.

DAY 55

Holding on sometimes hurts more. You are causing self-inflicting wounds physically and mentally.

Not realizing we cause our own pain. We set ourselves back and then we complain. Lessons are meant to be learned from. Grow and learn from your pain; the best teacher is self-taught. Move forward with confidence.

DAY 56

Dedicate your happiness to those who are happy for you, happy for your success and happy about life in general.

Surround yourself with those who will celebrate you. Be around inspiring individuals who will force you to become a better person. Success surrounds itself around success. Negative people despise positive people.

Week 8 Inspirational Journal

What daily habits do you need to adopt into your lifestyle?

_____

_____

_____

_____

_____

_____

What motivates you to keep going?

_____

_____

_____

_____

_____

_____

What pain are you inflicting on yourself?

_____

_____

_____

_____

_____

_____

List the people in your life that contribute to your happiness.

_____

_____

_____

_____

_____

_____

ARKINSPIRE
WEEK 9

"Success has nothing to do with what you gain or accomplish in life. It's what you do for others." Today it's me, tomorrow it can be you. Accept your Greatness."

DAY 57

You have to take you more seriously. The important things in your life, you must value.

Live, Love and Laugh. You matter! What you put the majority of your time and energy into, you become. Learn to value you and what life has to offer.

DAY 58

You may encounter many defeats but must not be defeated. You took some major blows in life. You are still standing.

The reason you are still standing is that you are truly a warrior. You are ferocious. You don't stop, you keep fighting. Never give in and never give up. You will have the victory.

DAY 59

The real test is not whether you withstand the test but whether or not if you learned from it.

Life will teach you many valuable lessons. Through every lesson, you must take all failures, hardships and develop from them. You must grow from them and most importantly continue to stand.

DAY 60

Your failures are not a mistake.
The real mistake is to stop trying.
"Never Stop Trying!"

Never give up and never give in, just trust you will eventually win. Just focus on the positive and not the negative. Your mistakes are a testament of your ability to not being afraid of trying.

Now that you have been Arkinspired, what are you going to do next?

_____

_____

_____

_____

_____

_____

_____

_____

_____

_____

SHOP OUR APPAREL AND LET THE WORLD KNOW THAT YOU LIVE TO INSPIRE

www.arkinspire.com/shop

ABOUT THE AUTHOR

*A*rkevious *"Arkinspire" Armstrong* is a motivational speaker, author, entrepreneur, mentor, and coach. While incarcerated he earned his GED and completed many educational programs, this allowed him to gain an earnest passion for empowering and motivating individuals about the importance of education by helping them make healthier choices and decisions in life. He earned his Associates in Business Management from Strayer University. Since being released in 2006, Arkevious has devoted his time to mentoring, community outreach and eventually starting his own program "Step Up To Leadership" a mentoring program for boys. He also has launched a clothing line, Arkinspire/Inspire Apparel for men, women, and children.

Made in the USA
Columbia, SC
18 December 2018